Anxiety: Top Tips For Rapid Relief Of Anxiety, Panic, Nervousness, And Worry.

DISCLAIMER NOTICE: This book is meant for general informational purposes only and should not be used to diagnose or treat any individuals. If you think that you or another person may have an anxiety disorder, you should consult with a medical health professional.

Introduction

I want to thank you and congratulate you for purchasing this book, *Anxiety: Tops Tips For Rapid Relief Of Anxiety, Panic, Nervousness, And Worry.*

This book contains proven steps and strategies on how to rid yourself of the heart-pounding agony of anxiety, whether anxiety is a new problem for you or you have suffered for years from this soul-draining psychological problem. Anxiety does *not* have to be part of your daily life, preventing you from the activities you enjoy, the people you care about or would like to meet, and the jobs that fulfill your unique talents. Whether you suffer from panic disorder, generalized anxiety, severe phobias, social anxiety or agoraphobia that restricts your life, there are good solutions to alleviate your anxiety. So read on!

© **Copyright 2015 by Lance Levan - All rights reserved.**

This document is geared towards providing exact and reliable information in regards to the topic and issue covered. The publication is sold with the idea that the publisher is not required to render accounting, officially permitted, or otherwise, qualified services. If advice is necessary, legal or professional, a practiced individual in the profession should be ordered.

- From a Declaration of Principles which was accepted and approved equally by a Committee of the American Bar Association and a Committee of Publishers and Associations.

In no way is it legal to reproduce, duplicate, or transmit any part of this document in either electronic means or in printed format. Recording of this publication is strictly prohibited and any storage of this document is not allowed unless with written permission from the publisher. All rights reserved.

The information provided herein is stated to be truthful and consistent, in that any liability, in terms of inattention or otherwise, by any usage or abuse of any policies, processes, or directions contained within is the solitary and utter responsibility of the recipient reader. Under no circumstances will any legal responsibility or blame be held against the publisher for any reparation, damages, or monetary loss due to the information herein, either directly or indirectly.

Respective authors own all copyrights not held by the publisher.

The information herein is offered for informational purposes solely, and is universal as so. The presentation of the information is without contract or any type of guarantee assurance.

The trademarks that are used are without any consent, and the publication of the trademark is without permission or backing by the trademark owner. All trademarks and brands within this book are for clarifying purposes only and are the owned by the owners themselves, not affiliated with this document.

Table of Contents

Chapter 1: What Is Anxiety?

Chapter 2: Therapy Can Help

Chapter 3: Using Medication to Deal with Anxiety

Chapter 4: Natural Remedies for Anxiety

Chapter 5: Complementary and Alternative Medicine for Anxiety

Chapter 6: Some Basic Do's and Don'ts for Coping with Anxiety

Chapter 7: Emergency Strategies for Sudden Anxiety

Chapter 8: Websites with More Information

Chapter 1
What is Anxiety?

Sandra's heart was pounding and her body was soaked with sweat. She was sitting in her seat on the airplane, and it was nearly takeoff time. Sandra needed to travel to see her extremely ill mother, and flying was the fastest way to get there. Sandra was frightened of flying, but she needed to see her mother as soon as possible. She felt like she was going to pass out, and must have looked ill, because the flight attendant came over to ask if she was all right. In a shaky voice, Sandra said she would be fine. And eventually, she was. She practiced her steady breathing and her relaxation exercises, and gradually began to feel much better. She still didn't like flying, but she knew she could get through it.

Everyone feels anxious and upset some of the time, particularly in the face of an object that virtually anyone would fear. For example, if a huge growling dog runs toward you and looks ready to attack, then you should be anxious! Or what if you suddenly see a very large snake or spider? Most people would feel very anxious under such circumstances.

Anxiety pumps up your adrenalin levels, and hopefully enables you to climb up a tree or otherwise escape from Cujo the dog, as well as from the scary snake or spider. Pathological anxiety feels just as bad (or even much worse), but it generally occurs when there is no real threat to you. Yet despite the lack of a valid threat, the doomed or frightened feelings, the racing heart, and the other symptoms of anxiety occur anyway when you have an anxiety disorder.

Many people having a panic attack like Sandra in the opening paragraph believe they are having a heart attack or a stroke, and they are extremely shocked when the emergency room doctor says it's an anxiety attack. In fact, a panic attack often closely resembles the symptoms of a heart attack, with an elevated heart rate, higher-than-normal blood pressure, and profuse perspiration. Fortunately, Sandra was able to use some strategies to calm herself on that plane to her mother who needed her. Read this book for how you too can resolve your anxiety.

Even if you don't have anxiety that rises to the level of an anxiety disorder, the suggestions in this book will help you during those times when you *do* become extremely anxious, such as on the day you are going to meet your partner's parents for the first time, just before you have to give a major speech, and on other occasions.

EXPLAINING ANXIETY

Anxiety that is chronic and severe is often referred to as an anxiety disorder. There are different types of anxiety disorders, but they are all characterized by an irrational and extreme fear and dread, and they are accompanied by physical symptoms, such as a rapid heartbeat.

Different Types of Anxiety

According to the *Diagnostic and Statistical Manual of Mental Disorders, Fifth Edition (DSM-5)*, a book published by the American Psychiatric Association, and accepted as valid worldwide by mental health professionals, the primary types of anxiety disorders are specific phobia, social anxiety disorder, panic disorder, generalized anxiety disorder, and agoraphobia.

Specific phobia

The person with a specific phobia fears a particular feared type of object, such as spiders or snakes. Of course, many people fear snakes and spiders, but the phobic person suffers an extreme fear that extends well beyond that of the average person.

Some phobias seem very silly to people, such as the fear of frogs (batrachophobia), of chickens (alektorophobia) or of bats (chiroptophobia). Most people don't encounter frogs or live chickens in their daily lives, and certainly you can easily avoid bats (unless you enter their caves or other locations where bats like to hang out). The phobia may become so intense that the person avoids large areas where they believe that the feared object might be, like a street, city, or even a province or state where the person once saw a frog, in the case of the batrachophobic person.

Social anxiety disorder (SAD)

Nearly everyone can remember a time when they had to give a presentation or speak up in church or elsewhere. The fear of public speaking is a nearly universal one. Organizations like Toastmasters help people to reverse their anxiety over speaking in public.

Social anxiety disorder (SAD) goes far beyond common everyday social fears. With this disorder, the person becomes anxious and fearful about interacting with nearly everyone, anywhere, with the exception of parents and very close friends.

He worries that he is highly likely to say something stupid or embarrassing, while she thinks that she might trip and fall down, and everyone will laugh at her. In fact, he and she can see such terrible events happening in their minds. The person is so afraid of doing something catastrophic that he or she foregoes nearly all social contact. As a result of this disorder, these individuals are often very lonely people. Therapy can help considerably.

Panic disorder

Panic disorder is characterized by frequent and chronic panic attacks. A panic attack is a type of debilitating anxiety that overwhelms and overcomes the person on a regular basis. She feels as if she is dying, although she might not know why she has this fear.

A panic attack is often accompanied by an increased heart rate and blood pressure, and many people in the midst of a panic attack think they are having a heart attack or stroke with a panic attack. Fortunately, panic attacks can be treated with deep breathing as well as with medication, herbal remedies, and many other options, all described in this book.

Generalized anxiety disorder (GAD)

If you have generalized anxiety disorder (GAD), you probably know that you frequently have an overwhelming sense of dread and impending doom, but you don't know what it is that you fear so much. This is a very scary and also a very frustrating experience.

For the person with GAD, almost everything is experienced as an "Oh, no!" event. Even if something wonderful happens, like you get a pay raise or fall in love with your soulmate, the person with GAD worries that this was such a great thing that happened, that it must be balanced out by some terrible event. This is not rational thinking and it puts a damper over the person's whole life. Fortunately, GAD is highly treatable, as are all forms of anxiety disorders.

Agoraphobia

The person with agoraphobia is afraid of being out in the open, such as being in the middle of a parking lot or a supermarket. (Or being in the middle of a supermarket parking lot.) They are often afraid of using public transportation because people with agoraphobia fear such closeness. Crowds are terrifying to the agoraphobic person.

Agoraphobia may prevent a person from having a job other than a home-based one, and consequently, they must prevail upon others to bring them food, water, and the other necessities of life. Even walking to the mailbox at the end of the driveway to retrieve the mail may be well beyond the capability of the agoraphobic person. Fortunately, agoraphobia, as with the other anxiety disorders, is treatable.

Who Suffers From Anxiety Disorders?

People of all ages and both genders may suffer from the sick feeling of anxiety that is present in all anxiety disorders, but some groups have a greater risk for specific types of anxiety disorders than others. For example, children are more likely to be phobic than adults, although many adults suffer from crippling phobias.

People with Specific Phobia

In general, the one-year prevalence of specific phobia is about 7%, which means that about 7% of the population suffers from specific phobia over the course of a year. The highest prevalence for specific phobia occurs among adolescents who are ages 13-17, or a rate of 16%. Fortunately, when phobic teens become young adults, the prevalence drops back down, perhaps because their hormone levels stabilize. In general, females are more than twice as likely as males to have a specific phobia disorder.

The person with a specific phobia may have had a frightening experience with the feared object, although this is not always true.

People with Social Anxiety Disorder

The annual prevalence for social anxiety disorder, formerly called social phobia, is about 7%, and this prevalence generally decreases with increasing age. For example, older adults only have about a 3% prevalence of social anxiety disorder in the course of a year. Perhaps their experience makes them less likely to be worried about what others think of them.

Most people with this disorder experience the problem for the first time before age 15. Social anxiety disorder sometimes may result from a bad experience, such as being bullied in school, while in other cases, the trigger for the disorder is unknown. Females are more likely to suffer from social anxiety disorder than males, in a ratio of 1.5 females to 1 male.

Individuals with Panic Disorder

Panic disorder is much less common than other anxiety disorders, and the annual prevalence is only about 3% among both adolescents and adults. Females are about twice as likely to have panic disorder as males. The onset of panic disorder is usually sometime after age 14. Younger children and adolescents can develop panic disorder, but it is unusual.

Individuals with Generalized Anxiety Disorder (GAD)

This disorder, which is characterized by constant worry and fear, has a one-year prevalence of 3% among adults and less than 1% among adolescents. Females experience twice the risk of suffering from generalized anxiety disorder (GAD) as males. GAD has its highest incidence in middle age.

People with Agoraphobia

This anxiety disorder is present in about 2% of all adolescents and adults. Females have about twice the risk for developing agoraphobia as males. Individuals older than 65 years rarely experience agoraphobia. In most cases, agoraphobia has its onset sometime before the person is 35 years old, and it rarely occurs in children.

MORE THAN ONE DISORDER IS POSSIBLE

Many people have more than one anxiety disorder, which can be very distressing to the individual. For example, a person could have social anxiety disorder along with generalized anxiety disorder, as well as other possible combinations.

In addition, many people with anxiety disorders often suffer from depression as well. People with anxiety disorders also have an elevated risk for developing substance abuse problems with alcohol or other drugs or with both alcohol and drugs. These problems may stem, at least in part, from attempts to self-medicate and decrease the effects of the anxiety disorder.

Alcohol or drugs may temporarily take away the anxiety while the person is under the influence—but it always comes back unless treatment occurs.

Chapter 2
Therapy Can Help

Therapy often helps people who have anxiety disorders, although the type of therapy that is used may vary. The most common form of therapy that is used today is called cognitive-behavioral therapy (CBT). This form of therapy helps people identify and challenge the irrational beliefs that are key to their disorder. However, some anxiety disorders are treated with exposure therapy, in which they are gradually helped to think about, and eventually face, the objects that they fear.

A combination of therapies may also be helpful, such as CBT and exposure therapy or other forms of therapy. Group therapy can help individuals with anxiety disorders considerably, because they learn that they are not the only ones suffering with anxiety, and thus they may feel less alone as others share their symptoms, their fears, and also their successes.

Cognitive-Behavioral Therapy (CBT)

Cognitive-behavioral therapy (CBT) is an evidence-based therapy, which means that research has shown that this type of therapy is highly effective in helping many people. Many studies have backed up this finding.

With CBT, the therapist talks to clients and learns what is going on in their lives. Once sufficient information has been gained, the therapist helps clients identify the key underlying irrational beliefs, sometimes referred to as though distortions. These thought distortions are causing major problems in their lives. Then the person learns to recognize thoughts expressing irrational beliefs and challenge these beliefs in her own mind.

One common thought distortion is an all or nothing thinking, also sometimes called black and white thinking. The person with this type of an irrational belief thinks that everything is either terrible or it is wonderful. There are no gray areas and no middle ground. Yet much of life really is sort of neutral—not fabulous and not terrible.

Catastrophizing is another type of irrational thinking that the CBT therapist helps a person challenge. The person misses breakfast, and may think, that's it, my whole day is ruined now. And her whole day probably *is* ruined, but only because of her irrational thinking, which will cause her to see everything through a dark and unhappy prism. The person with an anxiety disorder may take catastrophic thoughts to an extreme level, seeing death, severe injury or financial ruin around every corner.

The fallacy of fairness is a very common thought distortion, or the belief that life "should" be fair. People may think, I'm a good person, so why do I have this stupid anxiety disorder? The reality is that having a psychological problem is not related to being good or bad. Nice people have anxiety disorders and so do some not-so-nice people. Bad things happen to good people.

CBT therapists often may employ deep breathing and progressive muscle relaxation therapies to help their anxious clients. The reason for using these techniques is that the anxious person often experiences rapid and panicked breathing and an excessive tightening of the muscles. Read more about these two techniques in Chapter 6.

Exposure Therapy

Commonly used with phobic individuals, exposure therapy refers to a slow but steadily increasing exposure to the feared object. At first, the person learns to *think* about the feared thing, and in the course of thinking about it, she is trained to relax and calm her racing heart.

Later, if it is possible and practical, the person is exposed at a distance to the feared object, such as a dog or a horse. Of course if a person is deathly afraid of tigers, the closest they will get to this type of animal is within a safe distance from a cage in the zoo. Tigers really are dangerous, after all.

Interestingly, research has shown that when a person can relax while thinking about something that's normally scary for him (the phobic object), those relaxed feelings actually remain with him later on when he's at a safe distance from the feared object. It's as if both the body and mind have become desensitized to their former fear factor.

Keep in mind, however, that in times of extreme stress, the former phobia may recur, and exposure therapy will be needed again.

Group Therapy

Many people benefit from individual therapy, but group therapy can also be extremely helpful. When people who suffer from a common or related problem meet as a group, they learn that they do not suffer alone, as so many had assumed that they did. They also learn to share experiences and give and take suggestions from others.

Chapter 3
Using Medication to Deal with Anxiety

Prescribed medications are sometimes used to treat anxious individuals, although it's important to realize that medications have both their pros and cons. Xanax (alprazolam) is one anti-anxiety medication that you may have heard about before, because many people joke about it. In fact, this drug can be very effective in treating chronic anxiety over the short term. However, Xanax also can be habit-forming, and some people abuse this drug.

ANTIDEPRESSANTS

It would seem logical to assume that an anti-anxiety medication would be the first choice for doctors who are prescribing medications to treat people with anxiety disorders. But it isn't. Instead, usually antidepressants are used first to help people who are suffering from anxiety.

Most doctors who prescribe antidepressants for an anxiety disorder write prescriptions for medications in the selective serotonin reuptake inhibitor (SSRI) class of antidepressants. They may also prescribe medications in the serotonin norephephrine reuptake inhibitor (SNRI) class. These medications increase the level of serotonin (and also norephinephrine in the case of an SNRI). Both serotonin and norepinephrine affect mood, and more of these neurochemicals in the bloodstream work to elevate mood and also decrease anxiety. It's hard to be anxious when you feel good.

Some examples of SSRIs are Prozac (fluoxetine), Zoloft (sertraline), Lexapro (escitalopram), Paxil (paroxetine), Luvox (fluvoxamine), and Celexa (citalopram) Some examples of

SNRIs include Cymbalta (duloxetine), Effexor (venlafaxine), and Pristiq (desvenlafaxine).

Antidepressants may cause some side effects, such as insomnia, nausea, and diarrhea, as well as other side effects.

Some research has shown that people ages 24 and younger who take antidepressants may have an increased risk for suicide in the early course of their treatment. For this reason, the Food and Drug Administration (FDA) in the United States requires a "black box" warning on package inserts that caution should be taken. A black box warning is a highlighted and boxed warning with cautionary information about a drug.

BARBITURATES AND BENZODIAZEPINES

In the 1930s to about the 1960s, barbiturates were extremely popular drugs used to combat anxiety and insomnia, and there was also considerable abuse of these drugs. Seconal (secobarbital) and Amytal (amobarbital) were heavily prescribed in the early part of the century. Use of these drugs gradually fell off, at least in part because of the introduction of benzodiazepines, another class of medications. Barbiturates are still available today, but generally are not prescribed frequently.

In the United States, the Drug Enforcement Administration (DEA) labels both barbiturates and benzodiazepines as controlled drugs, because of their risk for abuse.

The Introduction of Benzodiazepines

In the 1960s, Valium (diazepam) and Librium (chlordiazepoxide hydrochloride) were the first benzodiazepines to be introduced, and they were immediately extremely popular. Benzodiazepines are anti-anxiety drugs. These drugs include the already-mentioned Xanax as well as Klonopin (clonazepam), Ativan (lorazepam), and Valium (diazepam), as well as others.

Benzodiazepines and Anxiety Today

People with generalized anxiety disorder (GAD) or agoraphobia who are prescribed benzodiazepines by their doctors are generally given such drugs as Klonopin (clonazepam) or Xanax (alprazolam). Individuals with panic disorder are more likely to be given Xanax or Ativan (lorazepam). Social anxiety disorder is often treated with Klonopin. People with specific phobia are more likely to be treated with exposure therapy than with medications, although anti-anxiety medications may also be prescribed.

OTHER MEDICATIONS FOR ANXIETY

Sometimes other medications besides antidepressants, barbiturates or benzodiazepines are used to treat anxiety. For example, the antihistamine hydroxyzine is sometimes prescribed for people with anxiety. In addition, beta blocker medications (often used to reduce blood pressure) are sometimes prescribed to treat anxiety. Some examples of beta blockers are Tenormin (atenolol) or Inderal (propranolol).

Although not used much anymore, sometimes older antidepressants are prescribed to treat anxiety disorders, including such medications as Norpramin (desipramine) or Adapin (doxepin).

Some doctors prescribe antiseizure medications to treat anxiety disorders, such as Depakote (valproate), Lyrica (pregabalin) or Neurontin (gabapentin).

Chapter 4
Natural Remedies for Anxiety

Mother Nature offers a variety of potential remedies for the chronically anxious person, and studies have shown that some herbal remedies may help you to resolve your anxiety, at least temporarily. For example, valerian is one herb that sometimes is used to treat anxiety, and chamomile is another. Lavender is also an herbal remedy, but it is primarily used as a form of aromatherapy, a subject that is covered in Chapter 5.

Before you take any herb or supplement for any reason whatsoever, first check with your doctor to make sure that it would be safe for you and will not interact with other medications that you take. Do not assume that because a drug is natural, that this means that it is also safe. Cobra venom is also natural—but you wouldn't want it injected into you.

You can purchase most herbal remedies in supermarkets or pharmacies or you may wish to order them online. Never take more than the amount recommended by your doctor or on the package. If the package says to take one pill a day, do not assume you'll feel better four times faster if you take four pills a day. When it comes to drugs, including herbal remedies (which act on the body similarly to drugs), more isn't necessarily better.

CONSIDERING CHAMOMILE

Chamomile has been used for many years to help people with stomach aches and diarrhea, as well as with anxiety. Some researchers at the University of Pennsylvania reported their findings on the effects of chamomile on people with anxiety in 2009. They found that chamomile significantly decreased the anxiety levels of their subjects, all of whom had been diagnosed with mild to moderate generalized anxiety disorder (GAD).

Chamomile is available as a tablet, capsule or a liquid extract or this herb can be taken in a tea. There are different types of chamomile, but most people favor German chamomile. Some people are allergic to chamomile, especially those individuals who are also allergic to ragweed or daisies, since these plants are related.

THINKING ABOUT GINKGO

Some research indicates that supplements of the herb ginkgo (*ginkgo biloba*) may improve anxiety in suffering individuals, although larger studies are needed to confirm this finding. This herbal remedy may cause stomachache, nausea, and diarrhea in some individuals. In addition, people taking blood thinners should avoid this herb altogether, because the blood may become too thin with ginkgo.

PURSUING PASSIONFLOWER

Passionflower, also known in Latin as *Passiflora incarnate*, is a plant that has sometimes been used to help people suffering with anxiety or depression. Passionflower is available in tablets, a liquid form, and as capsules. Research has shown some efficacy on anxiety with this remedy, although further research is needed.

According to the National Center for Complementary and Integrative Health, a federal government agency in the United States, passionflower may cause drowsiness. Of course if you have a problem with insomnia, as many anxious people do, you might consider this side effect to be a benefit instead of a side effect.

LOOKING AT ST. JOHN'S WORT

The herb St. John's wort, also known as *Hypericum perforatum*, is sometimes used to decrease both depression and anxiety. It is one of the oldest medicinal herbs known. However, some people may develop anxiety as a result of using St. John's wort. So far, only one small study in Germany found that St. John's wort improved anxiety, and as a result, much further research is needed.

It should be noted that St. John's wort reacts with many different types of medications, such as antidepressants, some heart medicines, and birth control pills, to name just a few. This is why it's very important to avoid this herb until you've first checked with your physician, received approval in advance, and you are aware of any possible interactions with other medications you take.

LISTENING TO LEMON BALM

Also available as a form of aromatherapy, lemon balm (*Melissa officinalis*) has been shown helpful in reducing anxiety in some small studies. Further research is needed. Sometimes lemon balm is combined with chamomile. This herbal remedy may be available as a capsule or a tea.

PONDERING RHODIOLA

Rhodiola (*Rhodiola rosea)* is sometimes used to treat anxiety, as well as headache, fatigue, and depression. The root extracts of this plant are available in capsules or tablets, as well as in a tea form. There is no research to date on the effects of Rhodiola on anxiety or anything else.

VALUING VALERIAN

Valerian, or *Valeriana officinalis,* is an herbal remedy that is sometimes used to help individuals suffering from anxiety and/or insomnia. However, there is not enough research to date to verify whether Valerian is effective in helping anxiety or not. This herbal remedy may cause stomach aches and headaches in some individuals.

Valerian is sometimes combined in tablets along with chamomile. Combined medications, even when they are "natural," should be used with caution. Never consume alcohol or take any other sedating drugs with any of the herbs described in this chapter.

LOOKING AT GREEN TEA

Some small studies have found that green tea reduces anxiety levels, but much more research is needed before green tea can be validated as a good antidote for anxiety. Keep in mind that green tea includes caffeine, so this substance could increase the risk for anxiety. There are some indications that the liver may be negatively affected by green tea. Further studies should provide additional information.

SEEKING SKULLCAP

Some limited research indicates that the Chinese skullcap plant (*Scutellaria baicalensis*) may have some anti-anxiety qualities, although further research is needed. There is also an American form of skullcap, also known as *Scutellaria lateriflora*.

The American skullcap is available as a liquid extract or a powder, while the Chinese skullcap is only available in a powdered form.

People with diabetes should avoid taking this herbal remedy because it may increase therisk for low blood sugar (hypoglycemia). This herb should not be taken with barbiturates or benzodiazepine medications or with any drugs used to treat insomnia. It should also be avoided in people taking anti-seizure medications.

NOT CONSIDERING KAVA

Some research has shown that kava (*Piper methysticum*) is effective in reducing anxiety, and this natural remedy is mentioned here because you may have heard about one of these studies. However, this herb has also been shown to cause liver inflammation and even liver failure. As a result, most experts believe that kava is far too dangerous an herb to use to decrease your anxiety.

COMBINATIONS OF HERBAL REMEDIES

Sometimes sellers of herbal remedies combine two or more herbs into one capsule or tablet. For example, as mentioned, a sleep remedy may contain both valerian and chamomile or other combinations of herbs. Always read the labels. If you are already taking sedating medications, such as an over-the-counter or prescribed medication that is sedating, stay away from herbal remedy combinations for your own safety.

Chapter 5

Complementary and Alternative Medicine for Anxiety

Some forms of complementary and alternative medicine (CAM) have proven to ease the stress of anxiety, based on research studies. Complementary medicine includes strategies that are not routinely used in Western medicine, although some doctors are favorable towards these methods. (Read about herbs that may ease your anxiety in Chapter 4.)

Here are some examples of several types of CAM that are used frequently to treat people with anxiety, and one or more of these options may help you too.

- Acupuncture
- Massage therapy
- Aromatherapy
- Yoga and tai chi
- Meditation
- Exercise

ANALYZING ACUPUNCTURE FOR ALLEVIATING ANXIETY

How could someone sticking pins into you make you feel less anxious? The process may sound pretty anxiety-producing instead. It's not entirely clear how acupuncture works, but it is known that acupuncture treatments help make some people feel less anxious. Some experts believe that acupuncture results in the release of serotonin and norepinephrine, which are two different neurotransmitters that work to elevate mood.

Researchers have found that acupuncture actually does provide some short-term relief for anxiety, although the jury is still out on longer-term relief. If you decide to try acupuncture for your anxiety, make sure that your acupuncturist is licensed, and has at least several years of experience in using acupuncture for anxiety.

MASSAGE THERAPY: IT IS RELAXING AND IT FEELS GOOD

Even if you don't have a sore back, neck or another aching part of your body, massage therapy can make you feel much more relaxed than prior to the treatment. It's very hard to feel anxious and distressed when your whole body seems to feel like one big sigh of contentment.

In one study at the University of Washington in Seattle, the researchers compared and contrasted the effects of three therapies. They analyzed the results of massage therapy, heat therapy and relaxation room therapy on individuals with generalized anxiety disorder. Interestingly, the researchers found that the anxiety levels of the subjects in all three groups improved significantly. However, there was not much difference in the improved responses of the people in the three groups when they were compared to each other. The researchers concluded that all three therapies included beneficial relaxation responses, thus decreasing anxiety levels.

AROMATHERAPY: SMELL THERAPY

Some people swear by aromatherapy as a great way to reverse anxiety and induce a state of calm. Research is mixed, but indicates that some people report experiencing a temporary relief from their anxiety when they inhale certain pleasant aromas emanating from essential oils. If anxiety were a smell, it would be very stinky and unpleasant. So it makes sense that smelling pleasant aromas could counteract your anxiety.

Lavender, with the Latin name of *Lavandula angustifolia*, is a pleasant-smelling herb used in aromatherapy, and it can relax people.

Lemon balm is another form of aromatherapy that has been found mildly helpful to people with anxiety. (And when you are very anxious, even mild relief may seem like a godsend.) Lemon balm may also be available as an herbal supplement.

YOGA AND TAI CHI

Using special movements under the rubric of yoga or tai chi can help relieve anxiety considerably, based on research studies. Yoga and tai chi are different forms of very specific types of exercises. Yoga includes stretching exercises that are combined with breathing techniques and meditation. Tai chi includes exercises in various increasingly difficult postures.

Many gyms and community centers offer yoga and tai chi lessons. To perform the movements correctly, you must concentrate and that means your brain can't fixate on how things are terrible and what if you get fired from your job—and so on.

MINDFULLY MEDITATING

Meditation is a process during which the person focuses on their own mind and body and ignores all outside distractions. Experts say that meditation can occur while a person is lying down, sitting or even walking around. Some studies have shown that meditation can decrease anxiety, stress, depression, and even improve some health problems. Community centers may offer lessons on how to meditate.

EXERCISING YOUR ANXIETY AWAY

It has been proven scientifically that exercising frequently generates endorphins, which are chemicals that make you feel better. It's also called a "runner's high" when the person experiencing it runs for exercise. In most cases, exercise will make you healthier and feel better—two great goals. Of course, talk to your doctor first before starting any exercise program.

COMBINATIONS OF THERAPIES

Many people use two or more forms of therapy to decrease their anxiety, such as combining exercise with yoga or tai chi, or aromatherapy with massage therapy. Try these different therapies and evaluate whether they work for you. If they do improve your anxiety problem, then consider making them a regular part of your life.

Chapter 6
Some Basic Do's and Don'ts for Coping with Anxiety

This chapter covers some basics on what to do and not do when you suffer from chronic anxiety, including actions you should give up altogether (such as drinking alcohol or smoking). You should also have an annual physical examination to detect any unknown health problems that may have cropped up and could be unknowingly increasing your anxiety levels.

Whenever possible, follow these basic strategies to decrease your overall anxiety levels:

* Avoid caffeine
* Don't drink alcohol
* Stay away from cigarettes
* Don't abuse drugs

AVOID OR DECREASE YOUR CAFFEINE CONSUMPTION
You may think that extra cup of coffee or tea will help calm you down—and you actually may get a little bit of a lift from consuming caffeine. However, in general, caffeine is not good for anxious people, and should be avoided. Caffeine is a stimulant , and people who are already anxious do not need more stimulation in their lives.

In general, a cup of coffee contains about 100 mg of caffeine, while a cup of tea may contain up to 60 mg of caffeine. A 1.5 ounce bar of chocolate contains 45 mg of caffeine. So-called energy drugs may include massive quantities of caffeine. It is also true that some over-the-counter medications may contain caffeine, as do some prescribed drugs. Caffeine speeds up the effects of the medication, which is why it is included in the drug.

This does not mean that you should give up your one (or three) cups of morning coffee right away. Suddenly ending a coffee (or chocolate) habit is likely to make you irritable and cranky, and also to give you a very bad headache. This happens because your body is accustomed to the caffeine boost, expects it, and needs it. Instead, try to taper off the caffeine slowly. For example, if you are a three cup coffee drinker in the morning, then taper down to two cups, and a few days later to one cup of coffee.

In one research study of students with severe headaches, the researchers found that all the students were very heavy consumers of caffeinated soft drinks. Once they tapered off the soft drinks, the chronic headache problem of the students resolved itself. Problem solved.

Anxiety isn't necessarily associated with headaches. But the point is, changing one habit can lead to positive consequences in your body. So slowly reduce your caffeine intake and see if your anxiety abates, at least a little bit. Odds are, you will feel much less distressed.

ALCOHOL: AVOID IT
Some research has shown that at least half of all the individuals who are treated for their alcoholism also suffer from anxiety. Many experts believe that alcoholics use the substance in a futile effort to self-medicate their psychological problems, such as anxiety and depression.

People who abuse or are dependent on alcohol should receive treatment to improve their physical and psychological health. However, the process of withdrawal from alcohol significantly increases the person's anxiety levels, which is why people undergoing withdrawal may be given anti-anxiety medications so that the process is more tolerable. Note that people withdrawing from alcohol should receive treatment in a treatment facility or a hospital, because of the medical risks of detoxification outside a treatment setting. There are many medical risks with a sudden withdrawal, up to and including death.

DON'T SMOKE
Smoking increases a person's overall anxiety levels, and should be avoided. If you have already started smoking—and many smokers started as teenagers—then you need to stop. Some research has shown that at least 20% of people who smoke also have anxiety disorders. Smoking also leads to many health problems, such as cancer, bronchitis, emphysema, and other serious health issues. If you already smoke, ask your doctor about treatments that can help you to kick this very bad habit.

You'll probably have some increased anxiety when you first start your anti-smoking regimen, but after your body stabilizes, your anxiety levels should be down significantly.

SAY NO TO DRUG ABUSE
Whether the drug is a prescription narcotic that is abused or it is an illegal drug, such as heroin, drug abuse increases a person's anxiety levels. Some people apparently self-medicate with drugs in a misguided attempt to decrease their anxiety. However, even if the anxiety seems temporarily abated, it will recur.

Some people abuse prescription drugs, including some anti-anxiety drugs such as Xanas (alprazolam). This is not only illegal, but it is also very dangerous to the body, and this behavior also can lead to a problem with addiction. When Xanax is combined with alcohol, as happens far too often, this can lead to a fatal interaction.

Although marijuana is increasingly accepted in society today, and even used to help some individuals suffering with severe chronic pain, research indicates that some individuals become *more* anxious with regular marijuana use, rather than more relaxed. Of course. if marijuana increases anxiety in a person, then that person should avoid using marijuana.

Chapter 7
Emergency Strategies for Sudden Anxiety

What if you're suddenly hit out of the blue with a bad bout of very severe anxiety, whether it's a panic attack, a phobic reaction, or another type of anxiety problem—and what if it's difficult or impossible for you to leave or to get any help? For example, if you're kayaking on your canoe down the rapids, and feeling very anxious, you may feel like jumping in the river to get out of there, but you know that you really shouldn't. For one thing, you might get sucked under the river and drown or you could hit your head on some rocks. Or both things could happen.

An anxious person can think of many other terrible scenarios that could ensue while they are kayaking down the rapids of a river. (And don't ask why on earth a very anxious person is kayaking in the first place! Maybe it was a bet that you lost.)

This chapter offers some simple strategies to help you get through some tough spots and deal with your anxiety, including such techniques as deep breathing, thought blocking, progressive muscle relaxation, and visualization. Practice these strategies ahead of time so you can easily draw upon them when you find yourself in a serious state of anxiety, and you want to recover fast, or at least decrease your level of anxicty to a more tolerable state.

BREATHE DEEPLY
Because anxiety that is caused by any anxiety disorder nearly always causes you to breathe more rapidly, one way to calm yourself down is to change your breathing pattern. When you breathe more slowly and deeply, your body will respond by slowing down. So what you need to do is to breathe in through your nose and breathe out through your mouth, taking deep

breaths each time. Concentrate only on your breathing and not on whatever is upsetting you. There is only you and breathing.

Eventually, your breathing rate will calm and you will feel better.

THOUGHT BLOCKING
Another way to decrease your overall level of anxiety is to stop your unpleasant or distressing thoughts in a hurry through the use of a technique that is known as thought blocking. For example, let's say that you have generalized anxiety disorder (GAD), and you start thinking to yourself in a catastrophic manner, "Oh no! If I fail this test, I'll never graduate. Everything I worked for will be gone!"

In this case, directly after a catastrophic thought, say to yourself in your mind, a loud "STOP." If you don't like the word "stop," then use "Halt!" or "No!" or another short and powerful word.

Every time the troublesome thought recurs—and it will recur—again say STOP in your mind. Eventually, your brain will listen and the bad thoughts will stop, at least for awhile. If they come back, use your thought blocking technique again. It can be very effective.

PROGRESSIVE MUSCLE RELAXATION
No matter what type of anxiety disorder you may have—if you've been diagnosed with any anxiety disorder—when you are in an anxious state, your muscles will tighten up in an automatic reaction to a real or perceived threat. This is the "fight or flight" response, and it's a very natural one. Learn this technique when you are not feeling stressed out, so you can use it when you are very anxious.

Once you have mastered progressive muscle relaxation (and it is not hard to learn), you can use progressive muscle relaxation when you actually are suffering from major anxiety.

To start with, lie down. You may start with your feet, thinking about them and then making the muscles in your feet very tight for a few seconds, then relaxing these muscles as much as you possibly can. Then with your mind, move into the ankles, and the lower leg muscles, tightening them so that they are tense for a few seconds, and then releasing all the tension out. Let it all go.

Move through your upper legs and to your abdominal area, and then into your shoulders and neck, arms, and hands and fingers. You will find that it is usually very hard to stay extremely anxious after you've completed a progressive muscle relaxation series. That's a good thing.

When you find yourself in a very anxious state, you can use progressive muscle relaxation. You don't have to lie down. You could be sitting in the doctor's waiting room and do these exercises. Just go through the body parts in your mind, first tensing them, and then relaxing them.

VISUALIZATION
Another good way to calm yourself in the midst of severe anxiety is to think of a very serene scene that you have previously imagined in a non-anxious state. It could be somewhere you have actually traveled or it could be an imaginary place. Fill it with unicorns and mythical creatures, if that makes you feel happy. It may also help to imagine water, such as a brook streaming over rocks or a beautiful waterfall.

When you visualize this scene, close your eyes so that you can "see" it in your mind. Notice details, such as what trees are present (if any), what the sky looks like, and create as many details as possible so that later you can draw upon this image when you are in an anxious state. Take a mental snapshot of your safe place and store it in your mind for future use.

Let's say that you need help right now, because you are starting to panic about your bills that were due last week, some really bad weather that's coming in (Oh no! A blizzard!), or something else. In many cases, at least several problems are really stressing you out.

Sit down, close your eyes, if possible, and recall your beautiful and safe place that you created in your mind. Let yourself feel its calming influence and tell yourself in your mind how pleasant and nice it feels. Don't let invasive and negative thoughts intrude because they are not allowed in your safe place.

If you're out in public and can't close your eyes, recall your serene vision inside your mind's eye. Think about the different aspects of the scene and admire them. It's hard to be anxious when you are enjoying true beauty—and what you visualize is beautiful.

Chapter 8
Websites with More Information

Everything there is to know about anxiety can't be covered in an e-book, and if you want to learn more, there are excellent websites online that can help you further. This chapter offers links to key organizations offering advice to the anxious. We've created hyperlinks for you or you can type in the site address yourself. We do not endorse any of these groups and you should check them out yourself.

AIM: Agoraphobics in Motion

http://www.aimforrecovery.com/

Anxiety and Depression Association of America

http://www.adaa.org/

Anxiety Disorders Association of Canada

www.anxietycanada.ca/english

Anxiety Disorders Resource Center

http://www.aacap.org/AACAP/Families_and_Youth/Resource_Centers/Anxiety_Disorder_Resource_Center/Home.aspx

Anxiety Network International

http://anxietynetwork.com/

Anxiety UK

https://www.anxietyuk.org.uk/

Canadian Mental Health Association

http://www.cmha.ca/

Freedom From Fear

http://www.freedomfromfear.org/

National Alliance on Mental Illness

https://www.nami.org/

National Institute of Mental Health

http://www.nimh.nih.gov/index.shtml

Social Anxiety Association

http://socialphobia.org/

Triumph Over Panic

http://www.paniccure.com/

Conclusion

Thank you again for purchasing this book!

I hope this book was able to help you to relieve your anxiety and live a happier life!

The next step is to continue to follow these recommendations and enjoy your life.

Finally, if you enjoyed this book, then I'd like to ask you for a favor, would you be kind enough to leave a review for this book on Amazon? It'd be greatly appreciated!

Thank you and good luck!

Check Out Some Other Books You May Like

Below you'll find some other books that are popular on Amazon and/or Kindle. Simply click on the links below to learn more about these titles.

When Your Adult Child Breaks Your Heart

Surviving Your Pet's Death

Fibromyalgia for Dummies

Feeling Good: The New Mood Therapy

Printed in Great Britain
by Amazon